Chronicles of The Butterfly:

Beauty, Resilience and Growth.

Uzoma Emmanuella

Table of contents

Definition of a butterfly:

Nectar-taking care of bug with two sets of huge, regularly brilliantly shaded wings that are covered with tiny scopes. Butterflies are recognized from moths by having clubbed or expanded radio wires, holding their wings erect when very still, and being dynamic by day.

Butterflies are profound and strong portrayals of life. Butterflies are delightful and have secrets, imagery, and significance and are a representation addressing otherworldly resurrection, change, trust, and life. The sublime, yet short existence of the butterfly intently reflects the course of otherworldly change and effectively advises us that life is short. Butterflies — We all know the outgoing person! This character is social and affecting. They must cooperate with others and are cordial, enchanting, enticing, garrulous, incautious, and hopeful. They are typically a decent pioneer and can persuade others.

Parts of the butterfly:
- Thorax
- Head
- Abdomen
- Antennae
- Probiscis
- Spiracle

HEAD:
A butterfly's head is brimming with critical organs that permit the butterfly to detect what is around it and to take care of it.
On the head, you will find:

RECEIVING WIRES (SINGULAR: ANTENNA):
Connected at the highest point of the head. Receiving wires are tangible organs used to get synthetic substances in the air, which might be anything from the smell of blossoms to the fragrance of an expected mate. They additionally assist with balance and distinguishing movement. Consider them the butterfly's rendition of a nose.

COMPOUND EYES:

Not at all like natural eyes, which each have one focal point, every one of a butterfly's compound eyes is comprised of numerous more modest "eyes" considered ommatidia, which each have their own focal point. The butterfly's cerebrum fastens the data from these minuscule eyes into an image of its general surroundings. Butterflies probably don't see the fresh, clear pictures that we see as people, however they compensate for it in alternate ways! Since the ommatidia in their compound eyes are completely pointed in marginally various bearings, butterflies can see advances, in reverse, above and underneath themselves all simultaneously. Also, butterfly eyes can see bright light, which people can't. This proves to be useful since certain blossoms and, surprisingly, different butterflies have extraordinary markings on them that must be found in a bright light.

PROBOSCIS:

The proboscis is the butterfly's mouthpart. It is utilized like a straw to suck up fluids, for example, blossom nectar, water, natural product juices, spilling tree sap, creature sweat, or different things relying upon the species. At the point when being used, the proboscis seems to be a little wire emerging from under the front of the head. At the point when not being used, it loops up firmly like a spring under the front of the head. Butterflies are simply ready to taste fluids with their proboscis and can't penetrate or break the skin.

CHEST:

A butterfly's chest is a stalwart that has all that a butterfly needs to move and zoom around its current circumstance.

On the chest, you will find:

SIX LEGS:
These are connected to the underside of the chest.
Each fragmented leg has 5 segments, however, the 3
that are not difficult to see are the femur, tibia, and
bone structure. Consider the femur the "thigh", the
tibia as the "shin", and the bone structure as the
"foot". A butterfly's legs have a similar capability as
our own, assisting them with climbing and walking.
Notwithstanding, did you have at least some idea
that a butterfly's foot likewise assists it with tasting?
Extraordinary sensors on every bone structure get
synthetic substances from the surfaces they stroll on,
which assists the butterfly with detecting
scrumptious fluids or distinguishing plants for their
caterpillars. This is one motivation to try not to get
butterflies whenever the situation allows - the
creams and synthetic substances we put on our
hands can be challenging for their feet!
For what reason do a few butterflies seem as though
they just have 4 legs? A few butterflies, including
exceptionally normal species like the Monarch,
seem to have just 4 legs. This isn't on the grounds

that they have lost two legs. These butterflies come from the family Nymphalidae or the brush-footed butterflies. All brush-footed butterflies in all actuality do have 6 legs, however, the principal sets of legs are really diminished, and are tucked against the chest and secret in the body's fluff. You will possibly see these legs on the off chance that you can cautiously pry them from the body with tweezers. These diminished legs have lost their capability in this group of butterflies, and are not utilized for strolling.

FOUR WINGS:
In spite of the fact that it might show up from the beginning that butterflies just have two wings, on the off chance that you have a more critical look clearly each side of the body has a forewing and a hindwing. The wings are covered with shaded scales, which are fundamentally minuscule straightened hairs that give tone to the wings. Butterfly scales are little to such an extent that without a magnifying instrument they simply seem to be shaded residue, and they are sensitive enough that they will get over right the wing on the off chance that they are scoured. Scales are one of a

kind to butterflies and moths, and they come in three assortments: pigmented, diffractive, and androconia. Pigmented scales get their varieties from shade synthetic substances they contain, which assimilate some light and mirror the rest. Over the long haul, color scales can blur, in light of the fact that in the end, the shade synthetic substances separate. For this reason, a few butterflies blur when kept in assortments that are presented to light.

Diffractive scales get their varieties by diffracting light, a comparative impact to utilizing a crystal to part white light into a rainbow. Diffractive scales radiate splendid metallic and brilliant varieties and don't blur over the long run since they have no color synthetic substances to separate.

Androconia scales will be scales that produce pheromones rather than variety. Pheromones are synthetic substances that butterflies discharge out of sight to speak with different butterflies of similar species, and are typically associated with assisting butterflies with tracking down a mate.

A butterfly's wings are utilized for flight, yet additionally have numerous different capabilities. Designs on the wings can assist with disguising the butterfly, caution hunters that a butterfly is harmful, shock or occupy hunters with ostentatious shows, and help a butterfly draw in and speak with different butterflies of its species. On account of harmful butterflies like the Monarch, the wings are additionally a magnificent spot for putting away poisons (however you would need to eat them to become ill).

MIDSECTION:

A butterfly's midsection may not seem to be a lot outwardly, however inside it holds indispensable organs that the butterfly needs to make due.

GASTROINTESTINAL SYSTEM:

The vast majority of a butterfly's gastrointestinal system is housed inside the midsection. This is where the butterfly processes food varieties and squanders.

SPIRACLES:

These are minuscule openings found at the edges of
the mid-region that let air travel into tracheal
cylinders in the butterfly's respiratory framework,
permitting it to relax. Not at all like us, a butterfly's
mouthparts are not engaged with relaxing! In spite
of the fact that spiracles may likewise be tracked
down on different pieces of the body, the vast
majority of them are situated on the midsection.

REGENERATIVE ORGAN:

Every one of the significant male and female organs
associated with multiplication is tracked down in the
midsection, situated towards the tip. The mid-region
is likewise where the eggs create and stay until a
female butterfly lays them.

It is beneficial to take note that a stinging butterfly
can't possibly exist. Butterflies have no stinging
organs or toxins in their mid-regions, or elsewhere
in their bodies. So don't stress over having a
butterfly land on you - they are totally innocuous.

Life cycle of a butterfly

EGG:

Eggs are laid on plants by the grown-up female butterfly. These plants will then turn into nourishment for the incubating caterpillars.Eggs can be laid in spring, summer, or fall. This relies upon the types of butterflies. Females lay a lot of eggs without a moment's delay so in any event some of them make due.Butterfly eggs can be tiny.

CATERPILLAR:

The Feeding Stage:

The following stage is the hatchling. This is likewise called a caterpillar on the off chance that the bug is a butterfly or a moth.

The occupation of the caterpillar is to endlessly eat. As the caterpillar matures it splits its skin and sheds it around 4 or numerous times. Food eaten right now is put away and utilized later as a grown-up caterpillar can grow multiple times their size during this stage. For instance, a ruler butterfly egg is the size of a pinhead, and the caterpillar that portals from this small egg isn't a lot greater. Be that as it may, it will grow up to 2 inches long in half a month.

PUPA:

The Transition Stage:

At the point when the caterpillar is mature and quits eating, it turns into a pupa. The pupa of butterflies is likewise called a chrysalis.Contingent upon the species, the pupa may be suspended under a branch, concealed in leaves, or covered underground. The pupa of numerous moths is safeguarded inside a cocoon of silk.This stage can endure from half a month, a month, or much longer. A few animal categories have a pupal stage that goes on for a considerable length of time.It might appear as though nothing is happening except for enormous changes occurring inside. Extraordinary cells that were available in the hatchling are currently developing quickly. They will end up being the legs, wings, eyes, and different pieces of the grown-up butterfly. A considerable lot of the first hatchling cells will give energy to these developing grown-up cells.

ADULT STAGE:

The Reproductive Stage:

The grown-up stage is the vast majority's thought process of when they consider butterflies. They appear to be extraordinarily special from the hatchling. The caterpillar has a couple of small eyes, squat legs, and exceptionally short radio wires. The grown-ups have long legs, long radio wires, and compound eyes. They can likewise fly by utilizing their enormous and brilliant wings. The one thing they can't do is develop. The caterpillar's occupation was to eat. The grown-up's responsibility is to mate and lay eggs. A few types of grown-up butterflies get energy by benefiting from nectar from blossoms

yet numerous species don't take care of the slightest bit.Most grown-up butterflies live only half a month, however, a few animal groups rest throughout the colder time of year and may experience a while.

Life span of a butterfly:

Butterflies are delightful and exceptional animals, however, they will more often than not have moderately short life expectancies. As a matter of fact, the longest-lived grown-up butterfly has a life expectancy of only one year.

Be that as it may, various types of butterflies can have different lifespans. Scientists for the most part concentrate on butterfly life expectancies and propensities by stamping them in the wild and afterward either recovering or locating them later and recording the information. While they can likewise concentrate on them in imprisonment, it is in every case best to concentrate on animals in their regular natural surroundings to get the most ridiculously complete image of how they carry on with their lives.

Butterflies in the wild are presented with a lot more risks and hunters, so concentrating on them this way provides researchers with a more precise perspective on how long they ordinarily live.

All things considered, most grown-up butterflies just live for around fourteen days. Some might satisfy six weeks, and the ones that relocate to additional heat and humidities might reside significantly longer before they get back to mate. Certain species can live longer than others. For instance, Monarch butterflies frequently live for a considerable length of time since they will relocate to hotter environments

Capabilities of the butterfly:

BUTTERFLY WINGS ARE STRAIGHTFORWARD:

Before you want to plan an eye test, let us make sense of it. The wings of a butterfly are canvassed in a large number of little scopes - a great many of them. What's more, those varieties you see when a butterfly flutters across your yard are the impression of different tones through the scales. The actual wings are comprised of a protein called chitin, which is the very protein that shapes a bug's exoskeleton. What's more, similar to an exoskeleton, chitin is straightforward. You've acquired some new useful information as of now.

BUTTERFLY WINGS HELP THEM AGAINST HUNTERS:

As we've examined, the life expectancy of the average butterfly is short, and even at their pinnacle are probably the most delicate. Remaining alive as far as might be feasible permits the butterfly extra chances to mate, and proceeding with the presence of its species is of most extreme significance.

Hence, butterflies habitually utilize their wings as a protection system. Either by collapsing to mix in with their environmental elements, or wearing a full range of varieties and examples to terrify hunters, a butterfly's wings are in many cases their best security. Butterflies have four wings, not two. Speaking of wings, we might have purposefully left the most intriguing butterfly truth until last! Despite how they might show up moving, or in drawings or artistic creations you might have seen, butterflies have four separate wings. The wings nearest to its head are known as the forewings, while those in the back are known as the hindwings. Because of solid muscles in the butterfly's chest, every one of the four wings goes all over in a figure-eight example during flight.

BUTTERFLIES HAVE A FLUID EATING ROUTINE:

We referenced before that butterflies like to eat, which is valid. What we did exclude at the time is that their wellspring of food is solely fluid. They just don't have the vital contraption for biting, truth be told. Utilizing their proboscis, what capabilities similarly you or I could utilize a straw, butterflies drink nectar or another variety of fluid food.

BUTTERFLIES JUST LIVE FOR HALF A MONTH:

For every individual who has been tensely anticipating this since our previous reference, or who essentially skirted ahead until they found it, here you go. The typical life expectancy of a grown-up butterfly is around three to about a month, be that as it may, the whole life cycle can endure anyplace somewhere in the range of two and eight months. Likewise, with anything, there are special cases for the standard. No less than one type of butterfly lives for around 24 hours, while a few transient butterflies, similar to the North American Monarch, can get by for almost eight months. Some butterfly species move from the virus.
Albeit by and large chilly climate will end the generally short existence of a butterfly by delivering them stationary, others accept the decreasing temperature as a sign to move. Butterflies are cutthroat and require - in ideal settings - an internal heat level of roughly 85 degrees to enact their flight muscles. If the weather conditions start changing a

few animal categories move looking for daylight. Some, similar to the North American Monarch, travel a normal of 2,500 miles!

THERE ARE JUST ABOUT 20,000 BUTTERFLY SPECIES:

Assuming that you'd at any point considered remembering every one of the different types of butterflies, it might take more time than you were expecting. A simpler beginning stage would be those species consistently happening in the lower 48 conditions of the US. In any case, that number is close to 575, so we're suggesting note cards or, maybe, zeroing in on the butterflies you track down in and around your yard this spring and summer.

BUTTERFLIES UTILIZE THEIR FEET TO TASTE:

If everything up until this point was at that point a piece of your current butterfly information, this reality might come as a curve. Notwithstanding, looking at the situation objectively according to the butterfly's perspective, isn't so surprising. A butterfly's everyday exercises comprise of eating and mating, the two of which require landing -

regardless of whether it is just momentarily. At the point when food is the need, those taste receptors assist the butterfly with finding the right plants and the key supplements it needs for endurance. Albeit many individuals can't help thinking about what it implies when a butterfly lands on them, truly it's most likely eager.

Functions of the antennae:

At the point when butterflies flutter from one blossom to another, they're not on irregular excursions. Butterflies have exceptional receiving wires that assist them with finding their direction, assist them with finding one another, and even assist them with giving the current time of day. Butterflies' receiving wires work alongside sensors on their feet as fundamental instruments that permit them to track down food, relocate, mate and rest.

SMELL:
Butterflies don't have noses, however, they have smell receptors on their receiving wires and legs. These permit butterflies to detect blossoms that are brimming with scrumptious nectar so they don't sit around idly arriving on blossoms that are unfilled with sustenance. The receiving wires' smell receptors additionally sense the pheromones of different butterflies, assisting them with making mates whenever the opportunity is correct.

CLOCK:

Butterflies will more often than not be dynamic during the day, resting when sunsets. Rather than simply utilizing their eyes to recognize day from night, butterflies utilize their receiving wires as light receptors. The receiving wires track the place of the sun and transform that data into a period of the day. At the point when butterflies lose their receiving wires, they can't decide time as well as those with unblemished receiving wires.

ROUTE:

One more key component of butterfly receiving wires is their capacity to assist the butterflies with flying in the correct heading. This is particularly significant in butterflies who relocate, for example, ruler butterflies. These gatherings should know which heading to fly during what season, like flying south for the colder time of year. This will in general work related to the clock highlight; to continue to fly south, for instance, the receiving wires should figure out what time it is and where the butterflies should be situated comparatively with the sun's situation overhead. This route framework additionally assists butterflies with finding their direction back to most loved taking care of grounds.

BALANCE:

The receiving wires can detect the bearing of the breeze and shifts in that course, assisting a butterfly with riding the breeze flows without getting lost or becoming bewildered. At the foundation of the receiving wires, butterflies have an extraordinary organ - - the Johnston's organ - - that draws data from the receiving wires to assist with keeping the butterflies adjusted. This organ assists butterflies with tracking down mates also, perceiving the wing beats of different butterflies of similar species.

Traits of a butterfly:

SHOW RESTRAINT:
 All beneficial things accompany time. We are developing, in any event, when we can't feel it. With extraordinary tolerance come incredible prizes.

BE AVAILABLE TO CHANGE:
Be changed. Without change, nothing lovely would occur. You need to surrender who you are to become who you may be.

BE LIGHT AND FREE:
Have a good time. Float from each entryway to the following. Search for variety, humor, and bliss in day-to-day existence.

BE UNCONSTRAINED:
Go any place your wings take you. Fly forward with certainty. Dare to immediately take advantage of new chances.

BE AT THE TIME:

Glance around. Partake in the blossoms, the sun, and the breeze. The current second is a gift for us to appreciate.

"Let's imbibe the butterfly spirit today".